D1288983

Abdo

JUN 0 5 2009

SCIENCE FICTION

YOU WRITE IT!

BY
JOHN HAMILTON

Published by ABDO Publishing Company, 8000 West 78th Street, Suite 310, Edina, Minnesota 55439.
Copyright ©2009 by Abdo Consulting Group, Inc. International copyrights reserved in all countries.
No part of this book may be reproduced in any form without written permission from the publisher.
ABDO & Daughters™ is a trademark and logo of ABDO Publishing Company.

Printed in the United States.

Editor: Sue Hamilton
Graphic Design: Sue Hamilton
Cover Design: Neil Klinepier
Cover Illustration: Background image, Don Maitz; Matrix photos, courtesy Warner Bros.
Interior Photos and Illustrations: p 1 Science fiction art, Corbis; p 3 Alien ships, Comstock;
p 4 Space banner, iStock; Futuristic man, Comstock; p 5 Writer thinking, iStock; p 6 Dog at
typewriter, iStock; p 7 Star Trek Enterprise, AP Images; Index card, iStock; p 8 Futuristic world,
iStock; p 9 Robot hand holding Earth, iStock; p 10 Handing holding pencil, iStock; p 11 Man working
outside on computer, iStock; p 12 Finger on keyboard, Comstock; *Star Wars* still frame of Luke
Skywalker, courtesy LucasFilm Ltd.; p 13 Index card, iStock; p 14 *2001: A Space Odyssey* still frame,
courtesy Metro-Goldwyn-Mayer; Alien hand, iStock; p 15 Darth Vader, Getty Images; p 16 *Star
Wars* poster, courtesy LucasFilm Ltd.; Alien face, iStock; p 17 Squid tentacle, iStock; p 18 Woman
thinking, iStock; Post-it note, iStock; p 19 Science fiction art, Corbis; Hook and question mark,
iStock; pp 20-23 *Star Wars* still frames, courtesy LucasFilm Ltd.; p 24 Woman celebrating, Comstock;
p 25 Spaceman, Comstock; p 26 Hand on mouse, Comstock; p 27 Computer and mailbox, Comstock;
p 28 *I, Robot* book cover, courtesy Bantam Spectra; *I, Robot* still frame, Twentieth Century Fox;
p 29 *Hyperion* book cover, courtesy Spectra; *Fahrenheit 451* book cover, courtesy Ballantine.

Library of Congress Cataloging-in-Publication Data

Hamilton, John, 1959-
  You write it : science fiction / John Hamilton.
    p. cm. -- (You write it!)
  Includes index.
  ISBN 978-1-60453-508-2
  1. Science fiction--Authorship. I. Title.

PN3377.5.S3H36 2009
808.3'8762--dc21
                                                    2008040266

CONTENTS

Introduction 4

Ideas 6

World Building 8

Work Habits 10

Character Creation 12

Plots 18

Rewriting 24

Get Published 26

Advice From Sci-Fi Writers 28

Helpful Reading 30

Glossary 31

Index 32

INTRODUCTION

"If my doctor told me I had only six minutes to live, I wouldn't brood. I'd type a little faster."

—Isaac Asimov

Science fiction is one of the most popular fiction genres today. No longer the domain of geeks and nerds, science fiction has gone mainstream. Ordinary people from all walks of life eagerly consume stories about time travel, space battles, killer asteroids, and robots gone berserk. There are many explanations for this, including the acceptance and popularity of movies such as *Star Wars* and its many spinoffs. Also, it seems today that we are *living* in a world of science fiction. Cell phones, planetary probes, powerful computers—all things that once sprang from the imagination of science fiction writers. Today, they are commonplace.

But that doesn't mean science fiction has nothing left to explore. New ideas are born every day. Thousands of science fiction books, short stories, movies, and TV shows are created each year. Perhaps *you've* got a science fiction story you're dying to tell. But where to start?

Novelist Gene Fowler once said, "Writing is easy. All you do is stare at a blank sheet of paper until drops of blood form on your forehead." What he meant is that writing is much harder than it looks. Anybody who can form a simple sentence thinks they can write. But good writing, like any other skill, takes practice.

Few people are born writers. Maybe you have a natural talent for writing dialogue, or know how to construct interesting characters. Or maybe you're great at dreaming up wildly inventive plots. But it's a rare beginner who can put it all together into a single story that succeeds where it counts most: entertaining your reader.

Don't let fancy literary terms get in the way of telling your story. Good writing takes practice (*lots* of practice), but there are certain skills anyone can learn. These "tools of the trade" can help you master the *craft* of writing. And once you've mastered the craft, you're well on your way to writing science fiction stories that others will love. You will encounter many obstacles along the way, but good writers find a way. The important thing is persistence, and a burning desire to tell your story.

Left: Good writing takes lots of time, practice, and patience.

IDEAS

As a professional writer, I've written dozens of books, novels, short stories, and screenplays. If there's one question people ask me the most, it's this: where do you get your ideas? The question is usually asked by insecure writers who are afraid they don't have the imagination it takes to be successful. I tell them not to worry—ideas are a dime a dozen. I've lost count of the number of people who, after finding out I'm a writer, have approached me with a *great idea*. They ask me to write the book for them, then offer me half the royalty money. Sorry, but it doesn't work that way. Developing an idea into a *story* is where the hard work takes place.

Still, ideas are important, nowhere more so than in science fiction. Science fiction writer and teacher James Gunn once said that science fiction is the fiction of ideas. And how exactly is science fiction different from "regular" fiction? Science fiction is often called speculative fiction. It's a place where you *speculate*, or make a reasonable guess, about how science will impact people. The key is that your ideas must be reasonably believable. This is called verisimilitude. Otherwise, it's just fantasy and magic, which is another genre entirely. Effective science fiction must be believable, although not necessarily accurate. It must at least have the *appearance* of being true.

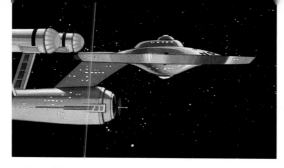

For example, the warp drive in *Star Trek* seems plausible. Any physicist will tell you that faster-than-light travel is not possible, but *Star Trek* uses scientific speculation to make it seem real. We know that when particles of matter and anti-matter collide, they produce tremendous amounts of energy. If this power could somehow be harnessed by an engine (*Star Trek's* warp drive), then perhaps we could indeed travel faster than light. Ridiculous, say the physicists. But we're willing to suspend our disbelief in order to allow the story to move forward. It's not scientifically accurate, but it *seems* possible. It has verisimilitude.

Coming Up With Ideas

- You must *read* in order to write. This is especially true with science fiction. Read a lot. Every day.
- Write what you know! Use your past experiences, then translate them into science fiction ideas.
- Brainstorm! Time yourself for two minutes. Jot down any ideas that pop into your head. Don't edit yourself, even if you think the ideas are stupid. They may spark even more creativity later.
- Keep a daily journal. It can be a diary or a blog, but it can also include ideas that pop into your head, drawings, articles, photos, etc. As you accumulate information, you'll see patterns begin to emerge of things that interest you the most. Explore these themes.
- Read scientific journals, magazines, and web sites. What interests you the most? How will today's scientific breakthroughs affect the world tomorrow?
- Write down your dreams. And your daydreams.

Common Science Fiction Categories
- Aliens (*The Left Hand of Darkness*)
- Time Travel (*The Time Machine*)
- Robots and Androids (*I, Robot*)
- Cyberpunk (*The Matrix, Blade Runner*)
- Space Opera (*Star Wars*)
- Hard Science Fiction (*Timescape*)
- Soft Science Fiction (*Fahrenheit 451*)
- Spaceships (*Rendezvous with Rama*)
- Future Societies (*Dune*)

WORLD BUILDING

A story's setting—where it takes place—is extremely important in science fiction. It establishes a sense of wonder, a critical part of the genre. Future societies are even more interesting when they inhabit strange planets out among the stars. In science fiction, creating these never-before-seen places is called world building. This is your chance to let your imagination shine.

In building your new worlds, don't just think about the physical location where your story takes place. You also have to create the rules that govern the society in which your characters live. For every special trait of your science fiction world, there must be consequences. This makes your story more interesting.

For example, let's say you create a society in which telepathy is normal. Take a step back and think of the consequences. How would you like it if everyone around you could read every thought that races through your mind? Would you be embarrassed? How could you ever keep a secret? Could you train yourself to focus your mind? What other consequences, advantages, or disadvantages would there be to living in such a world? These are the kinds of questions you must answer when creating your fantastic science fiction worlds.

Three Approaches to World Building

• Build from the Ground Up
Using your knowledge of science and astronomy, imagine the universe your characters live in. How big is the planet? Big planets have more gravity. How does this affect the story? What's the weather like? Does it rain water? Or acid? How many moons are there? How close is the sun? All of these choices will set the stage for your story.

• Continue a Trend
The world is faced with many problems today. Pretend what the world will be like in the future if things get worse. What will people do when the world finally runs out of oil? If war destroys civilization, what kinds of societies will arise? If computers become more and more powerful, how will people react if the machines evolve into a new life form?

• Alternative History
What if Rome never fell? What if Nazi Germany won World War II? What if dinosaurs never became extinct? These kinds of stories are a popular category of science fiction called alternative history. Think of your own "what if" and try to imagine what your new world would be like.

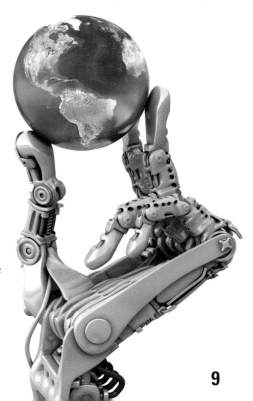

Engage Your Senses
When you describe your new world, don't just describe what is seen. Use all your senses. Is there a hint of sweetness to the air, or is it stale? What sound does the wind make when it blows through the trees? What is the taste of alien fruit? (Does it taste like chicken?)

WORK HABITS

"Work every day. No matter what has happened the day or night before, get up and bite on the nail."

—Ernest Hemingway

Established science fiction writers will tell you over and over, the only way to learn to write is to write every day. It bears repeating: write… every… day. You wouldn't hire a carpenter to build your house unless he or she had a lot of practice in the craft, right? Do you think Michael Phelps broke swimming speed records the first time he jumped in a pool? Of course not! He spent thousands of hours in the water refining and perfecting his technique before he won his first gold medal. Writing is like any other craft or sport: it takes practice.

Find your own special place to write, a place where you can work uninterrupted. You can't wait for the mood to strike. You have to make time, even if you're busy. J.K. Rowling famously wrote much of *Harry Potter and the Sorcerer's Stone* in neighborhood cafes. (Her baby fell asleep during walks, so she ducked into cafes to take advantage of precious writing time.) If you have a laptop, you might think you can write anywhere. But it's usually best to find a single place to write. A desk in your bedroom might do, especially if you can close the door.

Or maybe a corner table in the library, or a quiet nook in a coffee shop. Think of it as your home base. Psychologically, it will help you tune out the world and get down to the business of writing.

Friends and family can be a terrible distraction. Even a minor interruption can stall your creativity. Enlist their help by making clear to them that you need to be left alone during your writing time. It doesn't always work, of course. But as you become a more practiced writer, it will take you less and less time to recover from life's inevitable distractions.

Don't Plagiarize

Writers are creative people. They want to bring their own ideas to life and share them with the world. Sometimes, though, deadline pressure (or sheer laziness) causes people to plagiarize others' work. Stealing somebody else's writing is a terrible idea. Not only is it totally wrong, it can bring you serious trouble. You can be suspended from school, expelled from college, or fired from a job. Don't do it! Besides, the world wants to read what springs from *your* mind, not somebody else's.

Above: Find a place where you can write, then write every day.

CHARACTER CREATION

"First, find out what your hero wants, then just follow him!"
—Ray Bradbury

What's more important, plot or character? Some writers say plot. After all, your readers are expecting a good story. On the other hand, think of the best books you've ever read. Chances are, what you remember most are the interesting characters. What would *Star Wars* be without Luke Skywalker and Darth Vader?

The truth is, both elements are critical to good storytelling. You can't have one without the other. The reason characters are so memorable is because they are the key to unlocking the emotions of your story. You empathize with them, feel what they feel. Through great characters, you have an emotional stake in the outcome of the story. If you don't care about the characters, why should you care how the story turns out?

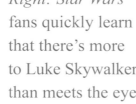

Right: Star Wars fans quickly learn that there's more to Luke Skywalker than meets the eye.

Character Biographies

Good writers are people watchers. Study the people you meet every day. Start a character journal; write down what makes these people interesting to you. Observe their physical characteristics and their behavior. What quirks do they have? How do they dress? How do they walk and talk? Mold and twist these traits into your own fictional characters.

Many writers find it helpful to create very detailed biographies of all their major characters. This sometimes helps you to discover your characters' strengths and weaknesses, which you can use later when you throw them into the boiling stew of your plot.

Backstory is the history you create for your characters. Most of it may never make it into your final draft, but it helps make your characters seem more "real" as you write.

Character Biography Checklist

Below is a list of traits you might want to consider for each of your characters. You should at least know this backstory information for your hero and main villain. What other traits can you think of that will round out your characters' biographies?

Character Biography Checklist

✓ Character's full name
✓ Nickname
✓ Age/Birthdate
✓ Color of eyes/hair
✓ Height/weight
✓ Ethnic background
✓ Physical imperfections
✓ Glasses/contacts
✓ Family background
✓ Spouse/children
✓ Religion
✓ Politics
✓ School
✓ Special skills
✓ Military
✓ Job/profession
✓ Hobbies/sports
✓ Bad habits
✓ Fears
✓ Hopes and dreams

Character is Action

Good characters are revealed through their actions. Instead of telling us that your villain is an angry scientist, show him pushing a little girl into a shrubbery on his walk to work. Okay, that's a little bit extreme,

Above: Good characters are revealed through their actions.

but you get the idea. The point is, it's always better to reveal your characters' personalities through their behavior. Let their actions speak for themselves. It's one of the basic rules of fiction: show, don't tell!

Viewpoint

Whose "voice" is telling your story? Most stories use one of two viewpoints: first person and third person. First-person viewpoint uses the "I" voice, as if the reader were experiencing the action personally. *"I opened the hatch of the spaceship and was greeted by a group of neon-colored aliens. What had I gotten myself into this time?"* First-person can be used very effectively to inhabit the thoughts and feelings of your main character.

On the other hand, third-person viewpoint (often called "third-person omniscient," or "the eye of God") lets you describe things your main character might not be aware of. You can describe your characters' feelings, but you can also take a step back and view the action from a more distant, neutral viewpoint. *"The astronaut opened the hatch of his spacecraft and poked his head out. Standing on the Martian soil was a group of neon-colored aliens. What had he gotten himself into this time?"* For beginning writers, third-person viewpoint is a good choice. It has fewer pitfalls and complications.

Short stories almost always use a single viewpoint throughout. In longer forms, like novels, some authors like to mix up viewpoints for variety. Varying viewpoints can be very entertaining, but remember to keep the same viewpoint in each scene. Otherwise, you'll confuse your reader.

Heroes

Your hero is usually your main character, or protagonist. He or she is the person the story is about. It's through the hero that your readers experience your science fiction world, and make an emotional connection with the other characters.

In science fiction, heroes are often larger than life. They go places and see things we can barely imagine. They don't just save the day—they save entire planets. But as you write, don't forget to give your heroes some flaws to overcome. This makes them seem more human, and interesting. Readers will root for a hero if they can relate to their fears and insecurities.

Villains

The villain is the antagonist of the story, the one who tries to keep your hero from accomplishing his or her goal. Villains can be great fun to write. Many science fiction villains are pure evil, but the most effective ones have weaknesses and motivations we can relate to. Nobody's afraid of a villain who's all bluster and anger. But create a villain who seems like someone we could bump into on the street, and you've created something special.

One effective technique is to make your villains charming. It's what villains use to lure their innocent victims, including your readers. Charm makes them villains we love to hate.

Right: Star Wars fans find the villain Darth Vader a much more interesting character as the story of his life is revealed.

Secondary Characters

Secondary characters are critical to how your hero overcomes the problems you throw in his way. Many types of secondary characters show up again and again in stories. Joseph Campbell, the great scholar of mythology, identified many characters who have common purposes. He called them archetypes, a kind of common personality trait first identified by psychologist Carl Jung.

Star Wars has many examples of archetypes. A *mentor*, or "wise old man or woman" (Obi-Wan Kenobi), gives critical help or knowledge to the hero (Luke). *Threshold guardians* (Imperial Stormtroopers, Jabba the Hut) hinder the hero along the way. *Tricksters* (Han Solo) are sidekicks and helpers who can be mischievous even as they help the hero.

How will you use your secondary characters? You might want to create character biographies like you did with your hero and villain. You should at least know what motivates them. How are they critical to the story, and why do they act the way they do?

Dealing with Aliens

Whether they are fantastic beasts or humanoids who can teleport at will, alien characters need to be thought out and consistent. For example, creatures from a large planet with crushing gravity would probably be short and squat. Aliens living on a gas giant might be wispy thin and light.

Fictional aliens are reflections of our human selves. They mirror our hopes and fears. By giving them human traits (such as fear, or hunger, or love), we can relate to them.

Alien language can be a problem. Handled the wrong way, it can grind a story to a halt. *Star Trek* used a devise called a Universal Translator. Or, you could have your aliens communicate using sign language. Or telepathy. Or some other means that only your creative mind can dream up.

Dialogue

Good dialogue propels the story. If you simply restate the obvious, then your dialogue is too "on the nose." After describing a hoard of aliens creeping over the horizon, you don't need your main character blurting out, "Look! Aliens are coming!" Instead, use dialogue to move things along. "Where's my blaster cannon? Don't tell me you lost it again!" In addition to giving information, good dialogue adds mood and suspense.

When writing dialogue speech verbs, a simple "he said" or "she said" is best. Too many beginning writers clutter their dialogue with unnecessary adverbs in order to show a character's emotions: *"Remove your tentacle from my arm," the astronaut said angrily.*

So, what's so bad about "angrily"? It's much better to *show* action. For example: *The astronaut swatted at the appendage. "Remove your tentacle from my arm," he said.* For a different mood, show a different action: *The astronaut recoiled in horror, his knees almost buckling. "Remove your tentacle from my arm," he said.* Two different reactions, but in each case the writer simply used "he said."

Start a dialogue notebook. Write down speech you overhear at home, during lunch hour, or at the mall. You'll quickly discover that real speech is very different from written dialogue. Real speech often overlaps, and is filled with "ums," "ers," and "likes." Written dialogue should not mimic real speech; real speech on the page quickly becomes tedious.

Write down interesting figures of speech you overhear. Idioms like "he threw me a curve" or "kick the bucket" can be great for creating interesting characters. But be sparing when writing regional dialects. A little goes a long way. And be especially careful when making up alien languages. If you use too many complicated alien words, you will lose the interest of your readers.

PLOTS

"Fiction is a lie, and good fiction is the truth inside the lie."
—Stephen King

Planning a piece of fiction, especially a long piece like a novel, can be a daunting task. It becomes more manageable if you break it down into smaller parts. You've probably already learned in school that fiction has three key elements: a beginning, middle, and an end. That seems simple enough. These are sometimes referred to as Acts I, II, and III. Acts I and III (the beginning and end) are critical pieces of the story, but are relatively short. Act II holds the guts of the story, where the majority of the action takes place.

Most English classes teach a pattern for fiction: There is first an exposition, where background and characters are introduced. Then a series of rising actions, where things happen to the main character. This builds to a climax, where the main conflict is resolved. Then there is falling action, where the story winds down. The very end is the resolution, where all loose strings are tied up.

While this basic information describes most fiction, it isn't exactly helpful to someone creating his or her own blockbuster. Where do you start?

Three Key Elements
of Fiction
Act I - Beginning—
Introduction
Act II - Middle—Rising
Action
Act III - End—Falling
Action/Resolution

The beginning of a story is called the "hook." How do you best hook your readers' interest? Many authors, surprisingly, don't start at the beginning. Instead, their books start with a bang, right in the middle of the action, with the hero embroiled in an exciting scene. Only after the scene's action is resolved do we take a step back and reveal the major characters and setting. One example: have your characters eject from a burning spaceship as they crash-land onto an alien world. Only after they've safely landed do you explain exactly who they are and what their mission is. Remember, character is action. By starting with an action scene, we automatically learn something about our main character. This is a common trick to snare your readers' interest, but don't overdo it. Make sure that first scene isn't too long and frantic, or else your readers will feel lost.

After the beginning, how do you establish the plot and tie it all together? In *The Hero With a Thousand Faces*, author Joseph Campbell described patterns

that are common to almost all works of fiction. These same threads have been woven into our stories for thousands of years. They form a mythological structure that authors use to tell the same basic tale, a story about a hero who goes on a quest to find a prize and bring it back to his or her tribe.

Some writers think it's useful to keep this "hero's journey" in mind as they dream up their own stories. Of course, you don't have to rigidly follow the structure. It is merely a guide. But if you really study the books and movies you enjoy, you'll discover many of the following elements hidden within.

Above: A classic plot sends a hero on a quest to find a prize and bring it back.

Act I

The Ordinary World

This section introduces the hero before the adventure begins. What does your hero want? What's at stake? When we first see Luke Skywalker in *Star Wars*, he's a simple farm boy. He yearns to be out among the stars having adventures, but he's stuck at home for now.

Above: Luke Skywalker leaves his ordinary world to join Obi-Wan, Han Solo, and Chewbacca in a great adventure.

The Call to Adventure

This is where some sort of event happens that gets the story moving. There may be a message or temptation that calls your hero to act. The message is often delivered by a type of character, or archetype, called a herald. In *Star Wars*, the droids R2-D2 and C-3PO are heralds. They bring an urgent message from Princess Leia, a rebel leader fighting against the evil Empire.

Meeting the Mentor

Sometime in the early stages of the story, the hero meets an archetype called the "wise old man" or "wise old woman." These mentor characters help the hero by providing critical background information, teaching special skills and wisdom, and perhaps giving equipment and weapons needed to complete the journey. In *Star Wars*, Obi-Wan Kenobi is the story's mentor character.

Crossing the Threshold

This is the point where the hero makes a decision (or a decision is made for him), and he's thrown into the adventure. A critical event called a plot point occurs. In *Star Wars*, Imperial Stormtroopers murder Luke's uncle and aunt. Luke realizes he can never return to his old life. He agrees to join Obi-Wan in the journey to Princess Leia's home planet of Alderaan.

Act II

Tests and Conflict

Act II is for testing the hero. What allies does she meet? What enemies? Who is the chief villain, and what are his goals? Does our hero act alone, or does she gather a group together, a posse?

Act II is a series of rising actions and mini-climaxes. In real life, events happen in seemingly random order. But in a good story, each event the hero encounters is connected, leading to the next ordeal.

Throughout Act II, the hero learns the special rules of his new world. He grows as a character, setting aside his fears and gaining confidence for the ordeal to come.

In *Star Wars*, Luke learns the ways of the Force. He and his band of new friends rescue Princess Leia and escape from the Death Star.

The Crisis

The crisis is a point in the story where the hero faces his most fearsome test yet, perhaps even enduring a brush with death. I call this the "dragging the hero through the gutter" scene. It's where the hero's faith in himself is put to the ultimate test. Then the hero makes a realization, or figures out a puzzle, and sets off for the final conflict. The character has grown because of all the adversity he's overcome to reach this point. This is another critical plot point upon which the entire story turns.

In *Star Wars*, just before Luke and the others escape from the Death Star,

Obi-Wan is killed by Darth Vader. Luke's heart is broken, but now he realizes that it is his time to step in and save the day, using his newfound confidence and skills in the Force.

Left: The chief villain, Darth Vader, threatens the heroine, Princess Leia.

Act III

The Final Struggle

This is the point in the story where the hero uses everything he's learned and faces the ultimate test. In the great majority of science fiction stories, the conflict is based on physical action. The final struggle is a fight of some kind. In *Star Wars*, it's the point in the story where Luke leads a group of X-Wing fighters to blow up the Death Star. Luke uses his intuitive powers of the Force to defeat the Death Star's seemingly invincible defenses, something he never could have done as a simple farm boy before he set out on his hero's journey.

A common technique to add suspense, especially in action-oriented genres like science fiction, is to add a "ticking clock" element. Not only must the hero overcome all odds and defeat the enemy, he has to do it with a deadline breathing down his neck. In *Star Wars*, Luke and his wingmen have only a few minutes before the Death Star is in firing range of the Rebel base of Yavin IV.

Above & Left: The clock is ticking. Can Luke defeat the enemy before the Death Star fires on his friends at the Rebel base?

It's always best if your character wins the conflict on his own, especially if he uses skills learned during the course of the story. Beware of having another character swoop in to save the day. This kind of ending is called a *deus ex machina*, a Latin phrase that means "machine of the gods." In some ancient Greek plays, a cage with an actor portraying a god inside was lowered onto the stage, where he would miraculously solve the hero's seemingly hopeless problems. You've probably read books or watched movies where a similar event happened: an unexpected person or situation arises and saves the day. This is what some critics refer to as a contrived ending. You've spent the whole story building up your hero with new wisdom and skills. Let him save himself.

The Return

In many stories, the hero finally returns to his normal world. He brings back a prize, a symbolic magical elixir that benefits his people. Maybe it's gold, or medicine, or simply

Above: Luke and his friends are heroes.

wisdom. In many science fiction tales, the prize is the fact that the hero has saved the planet. But whatever the prize, what really matters is how the hero has changed (or didn't change) during his epic journey.

To Outline or Not?

Many writers create outlines of their story, right down to a scene-by-scene description of the action and each character's part in it. Sometimes they use notecards, which can be shuffled around until all the scenes are arranged just right.

Other authors shun outlines. They start with an idea, add a strong character or two, and then let their storytelling sense guide them along the way. These authors argue that rigid outlines stifle creativity.

Great works of fiction have been written using both methods. But outlines provide a nice roadmap for beginning writers. You can make changes along the way, but at least you've got a guide to help steer your story toward a satisfying conclusion.

REWRITING

"It is perfectly okay to write garbage—as long as you edit brilliantly."

—*C.J. Cherryh*

So, you finally finished your story. Congratulations! Whether it's a short story or a novel, you've achieved something most people only dream of. Take a step back, celebrate a little, and then get ready for more work, because there's a truth that you will soon discover: writing is rewriting. Editing your work is a crucial part of the entire process.

Don't edit yourself until you've cranked all the way through your story. If you edit while you write, you'll find things you don't like. It will stifle your creativity as you struggle to make things "perfect." Get that first draft finished, then go back and edit.

First, set your story aside for a couple weeks, or at least a few days. Amazingly, with fresh eyes you'll catch mistakes that snuck under your radar the first time around. Your second draft will be better than your first. Your third draft will be an even bigger improvement. Edit and polish your story until it shines. How many drafts do you need? It depends on the story. Some authors do a dozen drafts, others are content with only one or two drafts of editing after the first. You're done when you know in your heart that you've written your story to the very best of your ability.

Examine your plot. Are the characters well formed? Do they grow and change? Most important, is your hero likeable? Does the hero have traits we admire? Can we identify with him or her? Do we care if the hero succeeds?

What about the beginning of your book? Does it grab the reader by the throat and never let go?

Are there scenes or events that are really necessary to push the story forward? Be honest with yourself. Be ruthless. Your story will be stronger the tighter you make it. Always, always remember your readers.

Keep your paragraphs short.

When appropriate, use active verbs instead of passive verbs. Instead of "Astronaut Spiff was bitten by the alien," try "The alien bit Astronaut Spiff." See how much more interesting that simple change made the sentence?

Make sure you keep one point of view per scene.

Read your dialogue out loud. Does it sound natural? Does each character have his or her own "voice"?

In your scene descriptions, be sure to engage all five senses. If you're describing a room, how does it smell? What background noises can the characters hear?

If you're a writer, then you know the importance of good grammar and spelling. By all means, spell-check your document using your computer software, but don't rely totally on its accuracy. There's no substitute for carefully proofing the story with your own two eyes.

GET PUBLISHED

"The reason 99 percent of all stories written are not bought by editors is very simple. Editors never buy manuscripts that are left on the closet shelf at home."
—John Campbell

Your story is written and edited—now what? There are many web sites that publish work by young writers. Do an Internet search for "science fiction webzines" to find reputable sites. Many of these web sites are also terrific places to learn your craft, with free advice from established authors. You won't get paid much (if anything), but it's a way to get your work seen by an enthusiastic audience.

Or, you could start your own web site and publish online yourself. Some authors post the first chapter or two of their books as a free download, then charge a small fee if the reader wants more. Other authors post their entire work online, happy just to receive reader feedback.

Other Options:

- School newspapers or yearbooks. These publications are always hungry for material.
- Local, regional, or national creative-writing contests.
- Creative-writing clubs and workshops. These are a great way to get feedback from other writers. They also give you practice in critiquing others' work, which will improve your own writing.

- Local newspapers and magazines are always looking for new talent, especially if they can get it for cheap. Still, you have to start somewhere, and it's a way to get your work read by a large audience.
- Self publish. With today's page-layout software, it's easier than ever to create your own publication. Make copies for friends and family.

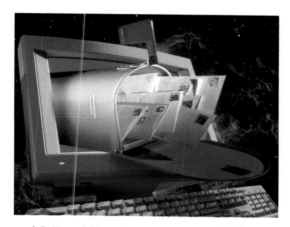

Publishers

If you are determined to have your story accepted by an established book publisher, first make sure your manuscript is ready. A clean, typewritten, double-spaced, mistake-free manuscript will go a long way in making your story stand out from all the rest. There are many "writer's guide" publications, some available at your library, you can use to research science fiction markets. They can also tell you how to write a query letter. Put your manuscript in a self-addressed stamped envelope (SASE), wish yourself luck, and mail it off. But please don't sit around waiting for a reply. Keep reading and writing!

Final Thoughts

If you receive a rejection letter, don't despair. Everybody gets them! Remember, the publisher isn't rejecting *you*, only your story. Maybe your writing isn't strong enough just yet. Or maybe your writing is fine, but the publisher isn't buying stories like yours at this time. Trends come and go in the marketplace, but don't try to write what you think publishers are looking for. By the time you finish your book, the fickle public will have moved on to the Next Big Thing. Simply write what you love, and the rest will follow.

You have the gift of storytelling. Sometimes you just need good timing and a little bit of luck. But remember, the more persistent you are, the luckier you'll get. Keep writing!

ADVICE FROM SCI-FI WRITERS

"You must keep sending work out; you must never let a manuscript do nothing but eat its head off in a drawer. You send that work out again and again, while you're working on another one. If you have talent, you will receive some measure of success—but only if you persist."

Isaac Asimov (1920-1992)

Dr. Isaac Asimov was one of the most popular and productive science fiction writers of the 20th century. When he was 15, his father bought him his first typewriter, for $10. Almost immediately, Asimov began churning out stories of fantasy and science fiction. Asimov led a remarkable career as a fiction writer. Over a span of nearly half a century, he wrote or edited more than 500 books, plus countless articles and essays. He's most famous for his *Foundation* and *I, Robot* series of tales. In addition to his fiction, Asimov had a gift for making science easy to understand. He wrote many popular books about chemistry, physics, and other scientific subjects.

Right: I, Robot was made into a movie in 2004.

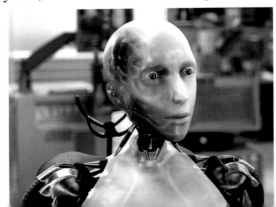

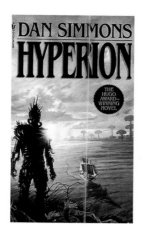

"Writers have words. Only words. From Aeschylus through Shakespeare to Dickens to Thomas Pynchon and beyond, that's all writers have in their tool box. That's all they ever will have. Words. The difference between the right word and the almost right word is the difference between lightning and the lightning bug."

Dan Simmons (1948-)

Dan Simmons writes some of the most thought-provoking, exciting, infuriating, stay-up-late, page-turning science fiction on the planet. He's best known for his 1989 debut science fiction novel, *Hyperion,* and its three sequels. Simmons masterfully weaves complex plots and themes into his novels, yet they are also spellbinding tales of adventure. The scientific details are utterly believable, but it is the human drama that is most memorable.

"How long has it been since you wrote a story where your real love or your real hatred somehow got onto the paper? When was the last time you dared release a cherished prejudice so it slammed the page like a lightning bolt? What are the best things and the worst things in your life, and when are you going to get around to whispering or shouting them?"

Ray Bradbury (1920-)

Unlike the "hard science fiction" of authors like Arthur C. Clarke or Isaac Asimov, Ray Bradbury's stories are symbolic, his writing often poetic. He uses familiar science fiction devices, like rocket ships and ray guns, but his themes include moral problems, lost childhood innocence, and how sometimes science, in the wrong hands, can be used to crush the human spirit. Ray Bradbury's most famous works of science fiction include *The Martian Chronicles* and *Fahrenheit 451.*

HELPFUL READING

- *World-Building* by Stephen L. Gillett
- *How to Write Tales of Horror, Fantasy, & Science Fiction*, edited by J.N. Williamson
- *The Complete Idiot's Guide to Publishing Science Fiction* by Cory Doctorow and Karl Schroeder
- *The Writer's Journey: Mythic Structure for Writers* by Christopher Vogler
- *The Hero With a Thousand Faces* by Joseph Campbell
- *Stein on Writing* by Sol Stein
- *Self-Editing for Fiction Writers* by Renni Browne and Dave King
- *Writing Dialogue* by Tom Chiarella
- *Building Believable Characters* by Marc McCutcheon
- *Zen in the Art of Writing* by Ray Bradbury
- *The Elements of Style* by William Strunk, Jr., and E.B. White
- *The Transitive Vampire* by Karen Elizabeth Gordon
- *Roget's Super Thesaurus* by Marc McCutcheon
- *2009 Writer's Market* by Robert Brewer
- *Jeff Herman's Guide to Publishers, Editors, & Literary Agents 2009* by Jeff Herman

GLOSSARY

Antagonist — Often called the villain, the antagonist is an important character who tries to keep the hero from accomplishing his or her goal.

Archetype — A type of character that often appears in stories. Archetypes have special functions that move the story along, such as providing the hero with needed equipment or knowledge.

Backstory — The background and history of a story's characters and setting. When writing, it is good to know as much backstory as possible, even if most of it never appears in the final manuscript.

First-Person Viewpoint — The "I" viewpoint, which makes it seem as if the person telling the story is the one who experienced it first-hand. "I grabbed my blaster and turned to meet the alien," is an example of first-person viewpoint.

Genre — A type, or kind, of a work of art. In literature, a genre is distinguished by a common subject, theme, or style. Some genres include science fiction, fantasy, mystery, and horror.

Hook — The beginning of a story, used to grab a reader's interest.

Plagiarism — To copy somebody else's work.

Protagonist — A story's hero or main character. The protagonist propels the story.

Speculation — To guess, or form a theory, about what will happen, without firm evidence. Science fiction is often called speculative fiction because its authors guess the future, usually based on trends they see happening today.

Third-Person Viewpoint — A detached, neutral point of view in which the story is told by an all-seeing narrator. "Han grabbed his blaster. Were those Vader's footsteps he'd heard in the hallway?" is an example of third-person viewpoint.

Verisimilitude — Something that has the appearance of being true, or real.

INDEX

A

Aeschylus 29
Alderaan 20
Asimov, Isaac 4, 28, 29

B

Blade Runner 7
Bradbury, Ray 12, 29

C

C-3PO 20
Campbell, John 26
Campbell, Joseph 16, 19
Cherryh, C.J. 24
Clarke, Arthur C. 29

D

Death Star 21, 22
deus ex machina 23
Dickens, Charles 29
Dune 7

E

Empire 20

F

Fahrenheit 451 7, 29
Force, the 21, 22
Foundation 28
Fowler, Gene 4

G

Germany 9
God 14
Gunn, James 6

H

Harry Potter and the Sorcerer's Stone 10
Hemingway, Ernest 10
Hero With a Thousand Faces, The 19
Hyperion 29

I

I, Robot 7, 28

J

Jabba the Hut 16
Jung, Carl 16

K

Kenobi, Obi-Wan 16, 20, 21
King, Stephen 18

L

Left Hand of Darkness, The 7
Leia, Princess 20, 21

M

Martian Chronicles, The 29
Matrix, The 7

P

Phelps, Michael 10
Pynchon, Thomas 29

R

R2-D2 20
Rebels 22
Rendezvous with Rama 7
Rome 9
Rowling, J.K. 10

S

Shakespeare, William 29
Simmons, Dan 29
Skywalker, Luke 12, 20, 21, 22
Solo, Han 16
Star Trek 7, 16
Star Wars 4, 7, 12, 16, 20, 21, 22
Stormtroopers, Imperial 16, 20

T

Time Machine, The 7
Timescape 7

U

Universal Translator 16

V

Vader, Darth 12, 21

W

World War II 9

X

X-Wing fighters 22

Y

Yavin IV 22

Right: Some writers really get into their subject!